My

Keep on expressing

your

Glow of

Grace

Love You, Girl!

Rev. Dr.

May Rose Thompson

09-06-2015

The Precious Pearl

Rev. Dr. May Rose Thompson

BALBOA.
PRESS
A DIVISION OF HAY HOUSE

Scripture taken from the New King James Version. Copyright © 1979, 1980, 1982 by Thomas Nelson, Inc. Used by permission. All rights reserved.

Scripture taken from the King James Version of the Bible.

Balboa Press books may be ordered through booksellers or by contacting:

Balboa Press
A Division of Hay House
1663 Liberty Drive
Bloomington, IN 47403
www.balboapress.com
1 (877) 407-4847

Because of the dynamic nature of the Internet, any web addresses or links contained in this book may have changed since publication and may no longer be valid. The views expressed in this work are solely those of the author and do not necessarily reflect the views of the publisher, and the publisher hereby disclaims any responsibility for them.

The author of this book does not dispense medical advice or prescribe the use of any technique as a form of treatment for physical, emotional, or medical problems without the advice of a physician, either directly or indirectly. The intent of the author is only to offer information of a general nature to help you in your quest for emotional and spiritual well-being. In the event you use any of the information in this book for yourself, which is your constitutional right, the author and the publisher assume no responsibility for your actions.

Any people depicted in stock imagery provided by Thinkstock are models, and such images are being used for illustrative purposes only. Certain stock imagery © Thinkstock.

Print information available on the last page.

ISBN: 978-1-5043-3463-1 (sc)
ISBN: 978-1-5043-3465-5 (hc)
ISBN: 978-1-5043-3464-8 (e)

Library of Congress Control Number: 2015909452

Balboa Press rev. date: 07/21/2015

God, help me to focus on truth, instead of trial. Help me to give thanks instead of giving into fear. Help me to choose joy instead of anger. Help me to trust your power instead of my plan. Help me elevate your name instead of my own.   Whitney Daugherty

2 Corinthians 3:17- Now the Lord is that Spirit: and where the Spirit of the Lord [is], there [is] liberty.   Kings James Bible

Dedication

I am so honored to dedicate these blessed and beautiful words of Spiritual Wisdom by the Executive Power of God, the Holy Spirit, my priceless gem. I praise God for sending the Holy Spirit to comfort, reveal, teach, and interpret the teachings of the Master Teacher to me, so many times.

To my mother, Warner Mary Gaines, now expressing free and unlimited in the spiritual realm. She taught my siblings and me, that we could be successful in life if we believed in the power of God. It took a while; however, she was right.

To the Reverend Doctor Johnnie M. Colemon, the founder of Universal Foundation for Better Living, Inc. and Minister of its mother church, Christ Universal Temple, Chicago, Illinois. President Emeritus. The teaching arm of the foundation, Johnnie M. Colemon Institute, provided the classes and instructors to open the way for so many to learn the Spiritual Word of Truth. Thank God I am one of them!

To my husband, Ford Thompson Sr., who has taught me so many things in our marriage of over forty years. He has taken every Johnnie M. Colemon Institute class with me, and taken every class I taught after becoming a Licensed Teacher of the foundation and our Church, The Living Truth Center for Better Living, East Cleveland, Ohio.

Ford believed in me as the Interim Minister of our church, when commissioned by, Rev. Colemon, when I did not believe in myself. It was he, who encouraged me to seek higher education, providing a multifaceted career. It prepared me for many opportunities in the ministry.

Ford permits the solitude I require to commune with the Holy Spirit, and encourages me to put into writing as received and instructed. Then, after reading the script he asks, "Where did you get this?" He knew it was not from me, but given to me.

I appreciate his faith in me as his wife, licensed teacher and his minister, and the co-operation and support he gives, then and now. Being a good and published writer himself, he assures me constantly, this is yours to do. Well, I have stepped out of my side-stepping shoes and surrendered, listening, and doing whatever Spirit reveals what is mine to do, that I may glorify, Father. So be it!

Table of Contents

Foreword

Rev May Thompson, "May", is an inexpressible, continuous, and unfolding blessing in my life. I thank God for her receptivity to his Divine Ideas. She has truly blessed and helped me sustain my faith. I have witnessed the same in other lives she has impacted. She is my spiritual mentor. She is a humble spiritual icon, a most dear loving friend, and I am honored to share this experience of life with her. Sharon Penro, RN UFBL graduate.

God is love and you are made in the image-likeness of Him. You are the very spirit image of Him. What do you mean you are not rich and beautiful? They don't call you great for nothing! Keep on expressing the loveable Truth about yourself. And so it is.   Rev. May Rose Thompson

The truth be told, others do not see the real you. In your spiritual self maybe you do look like; Mr. or Miss America!   Rev. May

Preface

O Lord, You have searched me and known me. You know my sitting down and my rising up; you understand my thought afar off. You comprehend my path and my lying down, and is not a word on my tongue, but behold, O Lord, You know it altogether. You have hedged me behind and before, and laid your hand upon me such knowledge is too wonderful for me; it is high, I cannot attain it. Psalm 139: 1 6

The Psalmist speaks of knowledge that God has for us. He speaks of God comprehending our path. He writes that such knowledge is wonderful, however, if we cannot reach it alone, how then shall we attain it? Is there somewhere we must go? Must we place ourselves in a certain position? Is there a special chant to utter? Must we humble ourselves to a special teacher that will come forth? If there is a teacher to access such wonderful knowledge, how are we to recognize this special teacher? Where do we go, if anywhere, and is there a special zone we should seek or, are we in it presently. The Master Teacher who taught the ancient teachings in the Holy Book, the Bible, made His Apostles aware that there is such a Spirit. This is your opportunity to become aware that perhaps this is your time to reach higher for the wonderful knowledge God has for you. You will find it accessible with the willingness to listen and surrender to the belief that it is possible and not complicated. If this is your time, there must be an effort to trust in the Higher Power to lead you on this path. Your pure desire will draw and lift you forward and higher. You will realize that there is a cost to its attainment and it is... tenacity and trust. Think not, that you are unworthy to enjoy this journey, the bliss, and the blessings. You are! It is a God thing. You were created for it! Trust the inner comfort moving within you as you begin to feel strengthened and free. Do understand that others may not understand you or what is going on with the change in your new direction. What will be going on is --- God going on within you. Remember this: when you experience the thunderous lift daily as you move to the awareness that you really do not have to go anywhere... you are already there. It's true! Right in the present moment where you are, you are in the zone of Love, and wherever Love is, God is. All you will ever need to achieve all the wisdom, and this wonderful knowledge is found here in your presence. It will unfold when you acknowledge the Presence here in the Sacred Sanctuary. Your heart has acquired the state of purity necessary to go and remain in the hills of the Lord and be taught. You are ready to give the ultimate offering, the cost, this being the greatest of all of God's creation...**Yourself**. You can do this! You will see! You will feel IT, the moment you recognize, accept, and embrace your Instructor...The Precious Pearl. I rejoice for you! In the Spirit of Love the Rev. Dr. May Rose Thompson

Today, keep on being loving, joyful, wonderful, doing good, and looking good, as a child of God should.   Rev. May

A good life is when you assume nothing, do more, need less, smile often, laugh a lot and realize how blesse you are for what you have.   Author Unknown

Be happy for the moment. This moment is your life.   Omar Khayyam

Acknowledgements

My love and gratitude to, the Rev. Loralyne Jones, my classmate, fellow minister, and friend for the vision to see greater things in me. She encouraged me so many times to pursue writing down the interpretations of the Bible that I receive. I am so glad I listened to her!

The precious prayer times I've had with my prayer partner, Dr. Vicki Turner are blessings from Spirit. Without fail we come together to pray for peace for the nation, the world, cities, and our homes. We have joyfully embraced this time together for (20) years and still going strong. I thank Father for you, Vicki.

The support from Vallery Bloom to me is immeasurable. I love and appreciate you.

Wanda Owens is my comrade in trying to solve the problems of the world. We have fun, discussions, and still not able to accomplish it.

My sister Florence still encourages me, wondering if I will ever sit still. No! Flossie.

Norma Powell; the Diva my life long sister in Christ. Bless You! It was her sister Shirley who gave me my Lessons in Truth Book.

I praise Father for His Holy Spirit. Nothing I do or have done has been successful without the Precious Pearl. I pray You will always reveal what is mine to do to glorify Father. God Is.

Always remember you are unique. So is everyone else. God loves it that way!   May Rose Thompson

God will never give you a problem you cannot solve. You are created in Divine Wisdom. You can solve anything. Be still and listen.   Rev. May

God is love and if you lose yourself in Him you will find yourself. Forgive, not because they deserve forgiveness, but because you deserve peace.   Unknown Author

Introduction

In the years of my youth, our family believed in going to church. We sang songs about how Jesus' loved us, because the Bible tells us so. After Sunday school, we went to the main chapel to the meeting of the congregation to worship the service. We called the chapel, "Big Church". There the lead singers were great at stirring up the emotions of some members and guarantee to heat up the service with praise and shouting. Our family said, "It was the Holy Ghost taking over. A ghost of any kind, holy or not was frightening to me. For years I didn't understand the difference between the Holy Spirit and the Holy Ghost. In my young adult life, I heard in Bible study about God the Father, the Son, and the Holy Spirit I heard, however, I did not comprehend.

In later years my desire was to understand who and what God is, His Son, and the Holy Spirit, and what did all this should mean to the Christian, and especially to me. My fear of not knowing prevented my attending Biblical studies to learn. A friend gave me the book, Lessons in Truth, by Emile Cady. And I read the book not fully understanding any more than before. However, this did encourage me to attend classes at the Unity Center Church. I did! There was enthusiasm stirring within for more in-depth study. I went to Unity Village in Lee's Summit, Mo. for the "May time Retreat" in 1972. It became the enlightenment I needed. I understood the necessity and importance to know the meanings of the biblical characters names and places, and, yes, of the Holy Spirit.

It revealed the importance of understanding the physical or literal meaning and metaphysical interpretation as well. However, it would

1

be the willingness to embrace the Teacher, the Holy Spirit, whom Jesus said would teach us, when he left this realm of existence. I prayed and meditated daily for the Teacher and received so much illumination, and interpretation of the spiritual Word of Truth. I began to find more revealing lessons in the scriptures, and how I was to make them a part of my life. I felt more energetic and began to see love in others. There was a desire, that projected from within me to become still and listen and. I began to long for these moments of silence more frequently; my life became more peaceful, joyful, healthy, and full of expectancy. Prosperity increased in accordance to my spiritual growth. Making my life one of belief in, "Practical Christianity." I came to realize the "Holy Spirit is God's Executive in Action". As a licensed teacher, an Ordained Minister, and Senior Minister of the Living Truth Center Church, in East Cleveland, Ohio, I learned you cannot build the Church of the Master nor have a successful ministry without the Builder…the Holy Spirit. My trust in Spirit as the director of my life has become most important. In the revelations here as you read, you, will become enlighten, too. The Pearl of … (A Great price") waiting to give you the …Kingdom of Good. Become willing to open your heart to learn. Allow yourself to be lifted into the hills of the Lord and experience the magnificent Teacher; I call my Gem, the Holy Spirit. It's simple, not complicated. Just embrace Spirit and be taught and learn the Truth. The Precious Pearl will embrace you and you will feel the Presence and will understand how very special you are to receive the gift of complete spiritual transformation. You can do this, you deserve it! I rejoice for you, dear one. May

Where I am

Where I am there is calm.
Where I am there is peace.
Where I am there is Light.
Where I am there is Love.
Where I am there is I Am.
Where I am is within.
And
God Is.
"And lo, I Am with you always, even unto the end of the world."
Matt. 28: 20. Amen

You Can do this

There is nothing like an idea whose time has come." You may have heard this many times, and been reminded that you, too, have had ideas. What happened? Did you think at the time, "I don't have any one to help me get it going? I don't have the money, space or the materials to get it started. Who will believe that I can do this, I don't even believe it myself. Right where you are an idea was born within you for the good of the world, an idea to make you successful and prosperous. And if you can believe this and remember the excitement when you received it and not allow doubt and excuses to overcome you, then you can exercise the faith within and let happen. More importantly, to grasp this idea is not only for you, but an opportunity to glorify God. And his God given idea is for you, and the potential is within you to fulfill it. This is your purpose, and you can do this. Accept this blessed idea and love it to perfection and manifestation. Claim it with gratitude! You can do this! Everything you need to start will be provided once you move out fear and doubt. In the book, The Science of Getting Rich, by Wallace C. Wattles, he gives an affirmation exercise to use for several days. It is as follows: "I can succeed!" All that is possible to anyone is possible to me! I do succeed, for I am full of the Power to be successful." Become still, listen silently again for the idea. It is a Divine Idea. Receive it and be grateful that you are the precious and special soul to have it. It's time has come and so has yours. You can do this! Remember, "I can do all things through Christ which strengthens me." Philippians 4: 13 "Nothing is impossible to God." Matthew 19: 26. You are not alone in this. Go ahead and say to yourself, I got this! I can do this! Yes, you can, dear one, yes you can!

Had times are blessings in disguise. Unknown Author

Entering the Love Zone

So many feel the need to seek love, somebody to love, and find something to love. There are those who try to understand why others cannot show or give us love, or what we think is love. Do we really have to go from place to place or person to person to receive love? Many a song or a poem has tried to elevate our understanding of love. There are many still looking for love, and trying to experience what they think or have been told what love is. Therefore, they are still seeking somewhere for it, when the Truth is that right where they are, they are in the zone of Love. The zone is right where you are, and the minute you realize that it is with you and within you, you are there. Your willingness to embrace the moment of stillness and enter the zone begins the end to the wondering about love and the beginning to experience bliss, joy, and beauty felt by the Presence of Spirit. In the Holy Book, the Bible, the scripture… 1 John 4:8 reads, for God is love. The Omnipresent Spirit of wisdom, power, life, and substance is the Presence of Love also, and therefore is everywhere present and within us as well. There is no need to keep seeking special places to go or special faces to find or situations that will let you know that Spirit is there. Where you are, you are there. Go within! And upon entering the Love Zone, you will find what no one can ever give you what you cannot experience yourself. When you embrace the moment, you will find all the love there is. You will find God. You will have found Love. You will realize that you have been there all the time. Go ahead, do it! This is your moment to intentionally experience peace, joy unending, and the realization there is no exit away from the zone. No way to fall out of love and no way to fall in love. You are part of It. And ye shall seek me, and find me, when ye shall search for me with all your heart.   Jeremiah 29:13

Happiness, true happiness, is an inner quality. It is a state of mind. If your mind is at peace, you are happy. If your mind is at peace, but you have nothing else, you can be happy. If you have everything the world can give, pleasure, possessions, power, but lack peace of mind, you can never be happy.   Dada Vaswani

Happiness cannot be traveled to, owned, earned, worn or consumed. Happiness is the spiritual experience of living every minute with love, grace, and gratitude.   Denis Waitley

Have enough trust to love, one more time.   Dr. Maya Angelou

I have been asked, are you wealthy? But, of course! How can one be a child of a rich Father and not be. Like Father, like child!   May Rose Thompson

I have learned silence from the talkative, tolerance from the intolerance, and kindness from the unkind, yet strange, I am grateful to these teachers.   Khalil Gibran

I have learned you cannot be a good Spiritual leader, or build a church, without the Holy Spirit.   May Rose Thompson

Purity

Oh, that I may dwell with the Lord, and stand in His holy place and Presence. There comes the time when one longs for solitude with the Presence; a time to move beyond prayer to feel God. Is that possible? Is there a time or place or both to embrace God, Spirit to Spirit? You might ask, why one would find the need to go beyond prayer? The effort to have the constant connection with Spirit increases the desire to fulfill this longing more and more. Satisfaction is possible, however, when purity in the Truth to know your God accelerates and nothing that anyone can tell or teach you gives satisfaction. It is a very personal experience. This longing is quieted only when you allow God to have His complete way with you. In meditation and prayer we do endear the moment, however, once experienced, there are no words to describe It. Only the magnificence and bliss causes one to want to dwell in this precious place time and time again. And since God is always present, His Presence is felt at the moment you surrender to grasp It. How does one know his or her worthiness to ascend and feel God at this height of expectancy? The Psalmist wrote "Who may ascend into the hill of the Lord. Or who may stand in His holy place? He who has clean hands and a pure heart, who has not lifted up his soul to an idol." Psalms 24: 3-4. We now understand why our teacher, Jesus of Nazareth in His "Be Attitude" sermon given on the Mount said, "Blessed are the pure in Heart, for they shall see God." Matthew 5:8. There is the need to lift our consciousness past time and understand, when we have the willingness to come to God with a pure intent, God is always ready to completely engulf us with His Presence. Acknowledgement of the possibility supports the ascension to the place within where we meet our Lord. You believe it can be done. Only one who is pure in mind, body and soul can see, (experience and know) God. This pure process leaves all concerns of earthly matters aside. Nothing is more important or meaningful any longer. Only this now moment! You are worthy, dear one, for Spirit longs to embrace you, too! You will feel It. You will know that this moment is different. You will understand King David's prayer "Create in me a clean heart, (mind), O God, and put a new and right Spirit within me." Psalms 51:10. When you have cleansed your mind of doubt, unforgiveness, unkind thoughts, selfishness; and demonstrate a spirit of unconditional love, faith and unselfishness, you are on your way. This steady and intentional purpose to build a spiritual consciousness; will take you to the site where you can approach the holy place with a pure heart. In this new Spirit you are ready and willing to cease everything that will stand in your way, and enter within to His Kingdom right where you are. You are now ready to see all of the glory of God. You are ready to feel God; you are ready to be blessed by His anointing. You will know when you are there, because you will feel Him, see His light, His warmth and His love. Allow Him to have His way with you. Stay in the Truth in your mind, and know in your heart that you are in the hills of the Lord. Stay there in the present, for therein lies His Presence. You will return there many times, because you will want to fulfill the longing, stirring within your whole being, waiting to be experienced and fulfilled. With a new spirit and a pure heart accept His anointing. Feel and know your God! "Man flows at once when the channel of purity is open."   Henry D. Thoreau

If you cannot see beauty in everything, you will not see beauty in anything. If you cannot see beauty in everyone you cannot expect others to see beauty in you. If you believe this is untrue, you are living a life of illusions.   May Rose Thompson

If you don't think every day is a good day, just try missing one.   Cavett Robert

It is hard to believe you are going anywhere when you are standing still for days.   May Rose Thompson

Kindness in words creates confidence. Kindness in thinking creates profoundness. Kindness in giving creates love.   Lao Tzu

Lord, let me be a blessing to someone today. Even in the smallest way. Let Your light shine through me and bring some type of happiness to their life.   Rev May

Many desire to understand the teachings of the Master of Nazareth; however, it cannot be done without, the teacher, the Holy Spirit.   May Rose Thompson

The Offering

I am not trying to change the world, I am just offering my gift that God gave me, and if somebody is moved by it, that's beautiful.
Lenny Kravitz

Omni presence, I honor you today with my offering.

Faithfully, without hesitation I give it to you.

Forever, I will always acknowledge the blessings you so willingly give me.

Endurance and forgiveness shall be the choices I make to stand before you.

Righteousness and love I shall see in others always.

Infinite One, I surrender In love the opportunity to serve you.

Need is not my experience, for you are my only need, and You are with me always as one.

Giving to you in joy, recognition, substance and time, I ask nothing, but your Holy Spirit to guide me to the worthiness to glorify you.

All that I have, I give to you from my heart, and it is the greatest offering I can give, and do give so willingly.

Myself. Use me!

It is the quality of our work which will please God and not the quantity.   Mahatma Gandhi

My trust in God flows out of the experience of his loving me, day in and day out, whether the day is stormy or fair, whether I'm sick or in good health, whether I'm in a state of grace or disgrace. He comes to me where I live and loves me as I am.   Brennan Manning

Silence is one of the great arts of conversation, as allowed by Cicero himself, who says, there is not only eloquence in it. A well-bred woman may easily and effectually promote the most useful and elegant conversation without, speaking a word. The modes of speech are scarcely more variable than the modes of silence   Tom Blair

I have learned silence from the talkative, tolerance from the intolerance, and kindness from the unkind, yet strange, I am grateful to these teachers.   Khalil Gibran

There are two ways of spreading light: to be the candle or the mirror that reflects it.   Edith Warton

Start by doing what's necessary; then do what's possible; and suddenly you are doing the impossible.   Francis of Assisi

Happiness cannot be traveled to, owned, earned, worn or consumed. Happiness is the spiritual experience of living every minute with love, grace, and gratitude.   Denis WaitleyThe

The Constitution only gives people the right to pursue happiness. You have to catch it yourself.   Benjamin Franklin

What's Going On?
Marvin Gaye

There are some important questions in the popular song that, Marvin Gaye asked when he wrote and performed "What's going on?" He sang about the war, the grief it caused mothers to cry and the sadness of our brothers dying. "What's going on? He had so many more questions and today we are asking the same questions. "What's going on in the world today?" We still wonder, if there will ever be something different, new and wonderful. Will there ever be peace in our world. Can we have a world of justice and love? No more hurt, crying, and needless dying? Will there be abundance for all and no more hunger or sickness? Why after all these years, these tragedies are still going? What is it? Many of us believe that we can give love unconditionally to all people. We believe that when we see oneness and perfection in each other as our higher Power does, we are on our way. We can experience peace, because we believe it is possible. We will surrender ourselves as peace keepers, peace seekers, and peace makers. It is possible, because many of us see and know it is possible. Hunger will cease, because the need will be filled overflowing. All will experience love because it is the natural, deserving blessing given to us. We will express love freely and without prejudice. There will be those who will believe it is a façade, and wonder what are we doing and what is going on? Those of us who know and believe the Truth will know what is going on. We have always known what is going on. The real deal about what's going on? What's going on? **God is going on!** And that's the Truth!

The weak can never forgive. Forgiveness is the attribute of the strong.   Mahatma Ghandi

Let no man pull you low enough to hate him.   Martin Luther King

When I do not know what to do, I pray and ask God what I should do. When I receive the answers, I do it.   Reverend Loralyne Jones

There is nothing as energetic as the anointing of the precious Spirt of God.   May Rose Thompson

My trust in God flows out of the experience of his loving me, day in and day out, whether the day is stormy or fair, whether I'm sick or in good health, whether I'm in a state of grace or disgrace. He comes to me where I live and loves me as I am.   Brennan Manning

God has put a Blessing on Me

"Our prayers should be for blessings in general, for God knows what is good for us." Socrates

When we learn the definition of a blessing, it reads as follows: A blessing refers to the infusion of something with holiness, spiritual redemption, favor and Divine Will. Wiktionary

Understanding the definition, we can admittedly feel and know that we have been blessed by a power higher than ourselves. And we have experience good that was given unto our own selves. How do we begin to speak gratitude for so many blessings? Just think about all that surrounds you. Can you see it as good and in special favor of God's divine will bestowed on you by the Holy Breath? The Holy Breath is blessing us in so many ways. Just think a moment of something that lives in our lives, and we may or may not give it a thought. Breath is a blessing. Inhaling and exhaling is a blessing. To be healed and express your maximum level of health possible are blessings. Mobility in different forms is a blessings Consuming and digesting are blessings. The ability to eliminate body necessities are blessings. Loving and receiving love are blessings. Receiving illuminations and wisdom are blessings. Giving and receiving joy, and gifts in return are blessings. Embracing life and expressing it fully is a blessing. Conceiving an idea, and understanding the spiritual Truth in it, and that your connection with love, and wisdom to bring that idea into manifestation, are blessings. Giving respect to one's parents and receiving respect as parents are blessings. Thinking, discerning thoughts, and making reasonable decisions are blessings. To be thankful to God for His love and redemption are blessings. Faith by man shall abound with blessings....Proverbs 26:20. Yes, God has put an abundance of His blessings in our lives and on us, and the Truth be told, those who know and believe it are expressing them well. We know them, feel them, accept them, express them, and the blessings are looking real good on us. Yes, God has put His blessings on us, and they are looking real good. Real Good! Thank you Precious Spirit for your blessings.

I give all the glory to God. It's kind of a win-win situation. The Glory goes up to Him, and blessings fall down on me." Gabby Douglas. Olympian Gold Medal Gymnast

There is no joy like the joy you receive in giving to others. It cannot be explained. Only felt.   May Rose Thompson

Surrender

Surrender fear for love

Surrender chaos for order

Surrender sadness for joy

Surrender to being whole for unhealthiness

Surrender hurt for comfort

Surrender to forgiveness and let go.

Surrender to inner peace and rejoice

May Rose Thompson

Nature knows just what to do and does it. Is humankind the only creation not fulfilling their purpose and potential?　May Thompson

A true friend is someone who thinks that you are a good egg even though he knows that you are slightly cracked.   Bernard Meltzer

You must be the change you wish to see in the world.   Mahatma
Gandhi

The Sacred Sanctuary

Today or any day you choose to sit quietly and just be still is always a good thing. However, today you may choose to sit on the patio, porch or deck with your eyes open or closed, and just observe, listen and feel the surroundings. Taking in the view, as you look out over the land, listen to the sounds, feel the energy, and gentle pressure of the vibrations becoming more apparent with the different fragrances marrying as the wind brushes across your face. You become aware of how radiant and lovely the day is as you notice the variegated colors displayed in the grasses. Some are growing tall and others low. The hedges are in bloom and beginning to progress to their full identity. The trees in their various assortments with blossoms are bursting through. Many have begun to bear fruit. Some filled abundantly, weighing down the branches as ripeness progresses. The branches take effect in such asymmetric designs any artist would be proud to paint. How quietly vines and flowers evolve into fullness ever so slowly and softly as each species develops into its specialty. Observe as the bumble bees in flight gently tap into each blossom employing their natural assignment and quickly return to their hive. The squirrels are jumping joyfully across the grounds up and down the tree trunks. You begin to hear the nuts fall with a light thud as the squirrels shake the tree branches. The bunnies have begun to multiply and are hopping along all over the place. Birds are flying about gathering what is needed for theirs nests. Just listen to their wings as they dart back and forth. Listen to their chirps of excitement and expectancy of their new generation arriving soon. See the flow and ripples in the pond with flocks of geese and their chicks following close behind. See the pond glow from the sunlight and hear the sound of the water softly rushing against the land. In the stillness you become aware that you hear the different vehicles move about the pavement, each with their distinctive sound. There is enjoyment experienced from the souls walking at their particular paces comfortable to them. How they laugh as they move along appreciating mobility, and the warmth of the morning. Above an airplane sounds loudly, however, the sputtering is not interfering the quiet moment as it continues to its flight destination. As the airplane flies on, the sound of the trees branches produces their own melody as the power of the wind moves them with motions of grace. One can feel the cool breeze of the wind embracing the body. Feel the fluttering of your hair as it brushes about your face. The stillness becomes apparent immediately when the wind ceases. Its stillness becomes so overpowering you become aware that the environment has moved you into another realm. There in the openness of the day, you have become so peaceful, ever so peaceful, that you have moved beyond the stillness to a perfect place. Right where you are, you have entered into the "sanctuary." A sacred and holy place. *You* have quietly witnessed, the Sacred Sanctuary of the universe. The Kingdom of God. "I will also meditate on all your works, and all of your deeds. Your way, Oh God, is in the sanctuary; who is so great a God as our God?" Psalms 77: 13:

The Reality of Freedom

All I have seen teaches me to trust the Creator for all I have not seen. Ralph Waldo Emerson

Truth in God gives us the freedom to express as a child of God. This belief in the Truth provides trust to walk the real path of love and peace, and as a child of God, this is as it should be. How do we begin? The Psalms of David encourages the following: Do not fret because of others lack of well doing. Trust in the Lord. Do well.

Walk in the land...Your mind, and feed on His faithfulness... the Word of Truth. Delight...Be happy and joyous in the Lord. Commit your ways to the Lord...Live Righteously. Rest in the Lord. Be patient and wait on the Lord. Do not fret, because the way others prosper. Cease from anger The Benefits of your diligence shall reward you the following: God will give you the desires of your heart. Commitment will bring all - good to you. You will experience righteousness as light illuminates your path. No harm will come to you, because you will not fret or worry. You will have justice in your life. You will inherit the earth. Delight in an abundance of peace. Your steps will be ordered by God, for He will uphold you. Psalms 37

We have the freedom and choice to live for the Glory of God. Just Trust and wait on the Lord, and enjoy receiving the desires of your heart.

When a Child of God Looks into the word of God And sees the Son of God He is changed by the Spirit of God In the image of God For the Glory of God Author Unknown

I shed my limited physical self and emerge with the infinite.
Sharon Penro

"Peace is a gift from the Divine and I acknowledge it as such. Always begin and end your day in a peaceful state of mind through speaking and listening to God. Listening is the most important part of the process."   Wanda C. Owens

I would rather live my life as if there is a God and die to find out there isn't, than live as if there isn't and to die to find out that there is.   Albert Camus

Proverbs 1:23: Turn you at my reproof: behold, I will pour out my spirit unto you, I will make known my words unto you.

To do and be the best is why we are here, but it is not easy

It is not because things are difficult that we do not dare. It is because we do not dare that things are difficult. Seneca

To be or not to be is not the question, we are all here for a reason. We have a purpose if we dare to claim it as our own. When we do, the idea and the plan we need becomes known to us. The idea can be developed, because the potential is there before the idea. Will we believe in the idea and its plan? That is the question. Should we or not? The decision must be made, but is not easy. Everything we need to fulfill any idea or desire is within us, because we possess the Power to succeed, and this is the best reason to get started. However, it is not easy. Many see it as just too difficult. Most of the time the answer is so simple, but the thought of it seems beyond logistics. It is just not easy. Trust in the Power that is in your entire being and realizes this is only for you to do. You must try, even when others seem to be advancing ahead of you, however, theirs will not be as yours, because their plan is given in accordance to their potential. Just believe and get started. It will not be difficult. You will find to do or not to do or to be or not to be is not the question. Try it that is the answer! It is not to apologize, To begin over, To be unselfish, To take advice, To admit error, To face a sneer, To be charitable, To keep on going, To be considerate, To avoid mistakes, To endure success, To profit by mistakes, To forgive and forget, To think and then act, To keep out of the rut, To make the best of little, To subdue an unruly temper, To maintain a high standard, To shoulder

51

a deserved blame, To recognize, the silver lining. But it always pays: try it. Anonymous

I can do all things through Christ, who strengthens me. Philippians 4: 13 It may not be easy, but I will try it.

If the Holy Spirit can take over the subconscious with our consent and cooperation, then we have almighty Power working at the basis of our lives, then we can do anything we ought to do, go anywhere we ought to go, and be anything we ought to be.   E. Stanley Jones

The Precious Pearl

Most gems are minerals formed over thousands of years beneath the earth. Pearls, however, are <u>born inside</u> the shell of the oysters beneath the sea. When foreign materials such as sand or particles enter the shell, the oyster produces and covers the irritations with circular layers of a solution called, nacre. There is about 7 to 8 years of this process. The result is the Pearl. The ideal pearl is perfectly round and smooth, but there are many other shaped pearls that occur.

The finest quality natural pearls have been highly valued as gemstones and objects of beauty for many centuries and, because of this, the word, 'pearl' has become a metaphor for something very rare, fine, admirable, and valuable. Natural or cultured the pearl is considered one of the world's most precious gems. Wikipedia

In the Holy Book of the Hebrews and Christians, the book of Genesis, writes in the beginning, the Master Creator, created perfect beings in His image-likeness. Many of us believe it. Male and female are perfect spiritual expressions of His remarkable love created to the giving, receiving, developing, doing, and of wanting nothing, but good. Provisions of delights and beautiful surroundings were abundance for them to enjoy and partake. The soul continues to experience the good that the, Master Creator, has in abundance for us, even today. Such supply shall never fall into scarcity, nor vanish, and is a blessings to all and not just to a certain few. However, there are those who feel undeserving, and believe they are born into this universe to live in a substandard manner. Many have believed that there is no hope in the ability to rise above this low maintenance of life, and therefore no effort is taken to seek a better life. Their true purpose of being is clouded by repetitive experiences of disappointment, lack, unfulfilled desires, and hope. How does one rise to seek the path and the truth to live a life that by grace they are entitled? There has to be a willingness to journey within the mind to bring forth the valuable desire to remove thoughts of seeming imperfections concealed by ages of false beliefs. Therefore, like the shell of the oyster, the process to cultivate the truth within begins with belief in the possibility. Remember, the pearl took years to be rounded into perfection. The main thing is to become aware that we are perfect, and no matter the past beliefs, it will take removing the sand, particles of doubts, and the smoothing out the rough edges of unworthiness to change them. The Apostle Paul, in his letter to the church in Corinth wrote…Remember, there us a natural body and there is a spiritual body. I Corinthians 15: 44 The natural body is made of dust, but the spiritual body is created in the Spirit. It is this spiritual change that, Paul likens to the teachings taught, by the, Master teacher, Yeshua Ben Yosef, known today as, Jesus of Nazareth. How then do we come to lift the Truth in ourselves? How do we change the inner rough edges in our thinking, to believing that we are worthy to be called the children of God? The standard of today's society requires much and it seems unreachable. There are two important requirements that must be considered and done:

There must be a sincere willingness to change, and rid the mind of false beliefs told to us for so many years, and many centuries. One must surrender to the task, now!

Secondly, Paul writes, again, this time to the church in Rome, that change is possible and a necessity, however, can be done only by completely being transformed in the mind, not by reforming, nor by conformation. Romans 12: 2. This transformation is possible and can be done only by the Holy Spirit. Then the change within the natural man can demonstrate the true nature of being. This Spirit, this Precious Spirit, is our (pearl of great price.) And the price is never out of reach, and is worth everything to purchase it. It is worth the opportunity to dwell in the spiritual perfection of the soul, and have everlasting peace, and good in the Kingdom of God, that is within us. The merchant, seeking pearly goods, found the great pearl and went out to sell all he had to purchase it. You will pay the price when you make the decision and be willing to start the process to transform and renew the way you currently think. Only the Holy Spirit can assist you in removing the sand...low (self-esteem,) and all false beliefs preventing you from inheriting the good you were created to have and express. The rough edges of doubt, forgetfulness, excuses, and the material particles that make it appear we are limited and undeserving are smoothed to reveal the Truth. And the revelation is that we are among most valuable of all creation. We are all beautiful gems, uncovered like the pearl produced by the oyster. Gems, all different in the way we glow, radiate, express our beauty, and yet are alike in that we are spiritual beings. We thank you, God for your precious gem that guided us to the renewing of our mind to the Truth. We thank you for your precious Pearl...the Holy Spirit.

The biggest trouble maker you will ever have to deal with watches you from the mirror every morning.   Author unknown

All major religious traditions carry basically the same message that is love, compassion and forgiveness the important thing is they should be part of our daily lives.   Dalai Lama

The Signature

There has been many discussions about handwriting. Today there are handwriting specialists that can determine the differences in writing, especially the signature. It has also been determined that as the personality changes, so does he handwriting. However, since ones signature is written repetitively, a greater effort is required to change it at a moment's notice. The signature is required for legal documents, which many times are witnessed at the time the document is signed. Today, the signature is related, not only in handwriting, but in the way we identify clothing labels, fashion designs, building structures, and fragrances. Some signatures are called logos, or emblems and symbols. Logos symbolize the design used by the company or organization on letterheads, and advertisement that can easily be recognized. The fashion designer, Anne Klein' signature is the lion, and is on the label of all her designs. Frank Lloyd Wright, the architect, always had a defining significance in his building structures. Businesses have logos which you recognize immediately when you see them. When you see the, Golden Arches, you recognize that this is where you can purchase burgers and fries, and not a Krispy Kreme donut. Tee shirts, shoes, beverages, handbags, and let us not exclude the hood ornaments of automobiles are identifiable. Countries are identified by the designs and colors of their flag. There is big money in the athletic sports businesses that generate tee-shirts, caps and other items with their logo on them. It is a million-dollar business. Fans just love it!

Those expressing sincerity in their spiritual lives, demonstrate the qualities that make the statement of what is believed. What we believe inside of us is lived outside of us, also. In expressing these qualities one will have to walk the talk, as it is said today. In other words, if one is really sincere about truly living a spiritual life, no matter the particular religion, it will be known by their deeds. The old adage, "Actions speak louder than words," comes to mind. There is no need to shout it out. Just live it! Jesus, the Nazarene teacher, taught that we are to express what we believe and likened the tree as the example what he meant. In the lives of those who are followers of Christianity should remember, He said, "Either make the tree good, and its fruits good, or else make the tree corrupt, and its fruit corrupt, for the tree is known by its fruit." Matthew 12:33. The apple tree will bear its signature...apples and not bananas. In our spiritual journey, we too, shall be known by our fruits. We will not have to shout out or convince others what we are about, we shall express our beliefs by living them and the world will know who we are by our fruits. The Apostle Paul wrote to the followers of the Church in Galicia, to remember the fruit of the Spirit. "They are, love, joy, peace, longsuffering, gentleness, faith, meekness, and temperance." Galatians 5:22-23. They will know you by your fruits--- your Signature.

Every thought, anything you produce, anything you say, any action you do, it bears your signature.   Thich Nhat Haiv

I love you when you bow in your mosque, kneel in your temple, pray in your church. For you and I are sons of one religion, and it is the spirit.   Khalil Gibran

If you realized how powerful your thoughts are, you would never think a negative thought.   Peace Pilgrim

Sooner or later, man has always had to decide whether he worships his own power or the power of God   Arnold K. Toynbee

Without accepting the fact that everything changes, we cannot find perfect composure. But unfortunately, although it is true, it is difficult for us to accept it. Because we cannot accept the truth of transience, we suffer.   Shunryu Suzuki

When the power of love overcomes the love of power the world will know peace. Jimi Hendrix

Love Lifted Me

Love lifted me, when nothing else would help, love lifted me. James Rowe 1912

The daily home to work and back was the responsibility for many, and most of the time was grueling. For most, looking forward to the weekend kept them going. Many a household looked forward to Sunday, the day to attend church to praise, pray, fellowship, and hear the message from the pulpit. No matter how hectic it may have been on the job or any other situation, there was great preparation and excitement looking forward to participating in the spiritual harmony of the service. Nothing moved the congregation as did the singing. Be it the choir or the soloist, the singing was the spark that made day. The rhythm and hand-clapping accentuated the mood and made worship so worthwhile. It was the music that energized the moment and made one forget the struggles, and for some the disrespect experienced on the job. The lyrics of many of those hymns seemed to be written just them. One such hymn was, "Love lifted me". No matter the valleys experienced, they believed that the love of God lifted them. No matter how grim the job environment or anything else had been, one could remember the song, "Love lifted me." Not everyone had the same situation; nevertheless, whatever the causes for feeling down, the song lifted them up again, and again. Perhaps for some it may have been relationships, other family matters, job loss, or the loss of a loved one. However, to hear those beautiful words were healing. The love of God, draws and attracts to us what is needed to lift us up. The love of God smooth's out the unevenness of chaotic circumstances. The hymn's lyrics touched the center of the soul with this stanza, "Love so mighty and so true, merits my soul's song! When nothing else would help, LOVE lifted me." Life can appear hopeless and burn away the ability to hold onto faith. Now is time to remember that all God wants and has to give us is His love and good. His love will harmonize the rocky road, and lift us up in spirit. We just need to trust Him! Yes, we did rejoice, praise, and sing those words from the old hymnal and meant every word. In many church services it is still a favorite. "Love lifted me, when nothing else would help, love lifted me!" God is love and love is God. God lifts us up when nothing else can or will.

LOVE is the only reality and is not a mere sentiment. It is the ultimate TRUTH that lies in the heart of the CREATOR.   Rabindranath Tagre

God is love and if you lose yourself in him you will find yourself.   Unknown

We are created in the Love of God and in His Loving Image.
We are just full of love, thus, have more love to give than you know.
May Rose Thompson

What if you were the one person in the world chosen to make a difference in the world today? Well? Get busy! May Rose Thompson

I would rather live my life as if there is a God and die to find out there isn't, than live as if there isn't and to die to find out that there is.   Albert Camus

What is there to lose in life without love? Everything! When, we don't understand the Truth. Love is not procession, love does not envy. Love is not conditional, but unconditional. Love is, I Am and I Am is Love. And I Am loves You!   May Rose Thompson

Everything has beauty, but not everyone sees it.   Confucius

Holding on to anger, resentment and hurt only gives you tense muscles, a headache and a sore jaw from clenching your teeth. Forgiveness gives you back the laughter and the lightness in your life.   Unknown Author

Surrendering to God is the most important part of your spiritual growth. You will Learn that, God is in command.   Rev. Charles Callahan

Need counseling? Need comfort? Need teaching and spiritual understanding? Need Anointing? Need lifting? Need answers to what is Truth? There is One ready to help you, the precious, Holy Spirit.   May Rose Thompson

Lord, let me be a blessing to someone today. Even in the smallest way. Let your light shine through and bring some type of happiness to their life.   Rev. May

There is nothing like a song sung with love and spirit to lift the soul. It is praise to God, and joy to those hearing it and the Diva singing it.   Norma Powell, the Diva

Trust

Trust that little voice in your head that says, "Wouldn't it be interesting if… and then do it."

Duane Michals There are so many reasons we put our trust in others. There are many reasons we trust the ability in our own selves to accomplish responsibilities and dreams. We trust in industry to give us safe products. We trust the warranties that support their product. We trust in many things regarding government, the medical media promoting medications, diets and exercises to keep us fit to live the maximum level of health possible. We delight in thinking that longtime friends and associates care about us and can be trusted. Oh! Yes, we can do most anything, because we trust ourselves without the help of anyone. Our belief level accordingly, raises our confidence of hope and expectation. However, sometimes we come to experience thoughts of failure, and disappointment in others, because we thought relatives and friends would believe in what we wanted to do, and give us encouragement. We quickly find reliance and trust in others is not always the thing to do. When the decision is made to fulfill an idea that we have received, we become aware that there is preparation needed to succeed. We intelligently move on the necessities to move toward the goal. We do the research and learn the requirements to support what we want to do. As we move along, there are those who really believe in us and others wonder and say, "just who told you that you could tackle such an idea?" However, the spark within us that brought forth the idea in the first place, energizes us to move forward. Once we understand what is necessary and take the first step, this Power gives us confidence and the feeling that we can trust IT. We begin to draw reliance and faith in ourselves and IT. Excitement lifts and motivates us to carry on no matter what is to be done or how long it will take to do it. We start the course, read the books, listen to the tapes, do the lessons, take the exams, and listen carefully to the instructors. Oh! Yes, we remember to pray and medicate and give thanks for every accomplishment daily. However, there are times we are confronted with challenges not listed in the course. We become aware there are those that test our patience and tenacity. They cause us to doubt and give cause for uncertainty. Many, however, no matter how few the comments, begin words of discouragement. Words that cause disbelief in the ability to achieve, and the hope and desire to continue is deflated. The negative remarks pierce the will. The drive and power to succeed fail at a time when faith should be prevalent and foremost in the mind and heart. At this time, you began to feel the wind blowing vigorously and the clouds forming, lightening sends the sound of thunder causing suspicion that a storm is on the way. You have allowed doubt to come and rain on your dream. Great strength is needed to realize that this is the time you don't have the answers. You believed you alone could do anything. Now you believe you can do this, too, without anyone. You can stop the storm! You had answers to everything and could make decisions rapidly. Now, you have listened to others and yourself, and nothing is working. This time, the storm is raining hail the size of golf balls upon you. Now what are you going to do? Others helped you to get into this raging problem and left you to defend for yourself. Who can you trust now? Who can you trust to bring out the sun, the light, and wisdom into your tornadic situation? If there is a moment of light trying to peek through the clouds, this is the perfect time to stop trying to figure it out and become still. It is the perfect time to listen, and this is the perfect time to remember the wisdom in the scripture, King Solomon wrote in the Proverbs. "Trust in the Lord with all your heart, and lean not in your own understanding. In all your ways acknowledge Him, and He shall direct your paths." Proverbs 3: 5, 6. Now, is the time to remember, that the idea you embraced did not come forth from you, it came from within you. The power to calm the storm of the situation is not in your hands. You have no power to move it, even when you have been a part of its gathering and coming upon you. When you stop leaning to the right and left in confusion, it is time to understand, that Divine Wisdom is at hand to clear the clouds. You realize you are in the way and can't see your way. Clarity happens when God is acknowledged and the way can be seen. Now you understand you're empowered by the giver of the idea. The path is corrected and directed for you. You can proceed! When you feel so alone; hear God whispering to you, "Trust me!" In the shadow of doubt and confusion hear Him say; "Trust me!" Eliminate immediately the moment you experience feeling overwhelmed and remember, He is calling out to you, "Trust me". When you come to the fork in the road, respond to His powerful words of Truth, "Trust me." I will direct your path, "Trust me!" Acknowledge Him and He shall, not maybe, will speak the Spiritual words of Truth and calm the waters so you will sink no further. Now you can continue your chosen destination smoothly. You can follow Him faithfully knowing He will direct you and be your companion all of the way. Have trust in the Lord, and do well. Psalm 37: 3. Still I will follow you Still I will follow you Still I will listen to your every calling While the storm rages on And I can't find my way Still I will Trust you Lord. Song and lyrics written by Vonnie Ewing Lopez

Without accepting the fact that everything changes, we cannot find perfect composure. But unfortunately, although it is true, it is difficult for us to accept it. Because we cannot accept the truth of transience, we suffer.   Shunryu Suzuki

The only reason for time is so everything does not happen at once.   Albert Einstein

Give me Strength

God our Creator, has stored within our minds and personalities great strength and ability. Prayer helps us tap and develop these powers. Author unknown

This is the day which the Lord has made, we will rejoice and be glad in it. Psalms 118: 24. So writes the Psalmist, however beautiful this day is, for some and maybe you, it is not lovely. The brilliance of the morning gives no spark of joy that there is a reason to rejoice. Everything about this day from the start has made some feel as if driving in the wrong lane. It makes you want to yell out, is it going to be this kind of day? Instead, call out to the Creator of this day, "Give me strength!" There are no clouds in the sky, but there are problems raining down on many. Namely me! Speak out again, to the maker of this day, "Give me strength*!* "In the race of getting to your destination through the hectic traffic, time is chipping at every effort to arrive there timely. Declare again, "Give me strength and patience!" Yes, in this lovely day, you are witnessing excitement and joy moving about in the lives of others, however, there is no seeming balance making its way in your path. In a firm voice, speak, "Give me the strength of peace and balance. Now!" In a day when beauty of the Lord's Day should be a blessed opportunity of enjoyment, the weight of confusion, pressures, challenges and disagreements with others and in situations prevents moving steadfastly in the lane and path of life you have chosen to travel. You think to yourself that you have tons of requirements and decisions to make that no weight lifter could lift aside. It is at this time you feel that you just do not have the strength to move around, above or out of the way of them. This is the time to realize there is no one on this earth with the muscular physique to flex his or her muscles to remove the weight of stress from your shoulders.

The solution needed will not come in a physical manner. No matter the situation, the answer is never found externally. If so, the answer would have presented itself. The solution needed lies within us. It is Spiritual, quietly waiting to be acknowledged, trusted and called upon. When we can collect our thoughts and remember that we are never alone, and right where we are is all the strength we will ever need. This Spiritual strength has the world on Its shoulders. We should never allow challenges, which appear to us as strong as raging winds to blur our opportunity to enjoy the day. Accept everyday as a blessing from God. If you feel the whirlwinds coming upon you, affirm, "I will call upon the Lord, my God, my strength, in whom I will trust." Psalms 18:1-3. Calm down! Call on the Lord! "God is my strength and power and He maketh my way Perfect!" II Samuel 22:33 Whatever you have allowed to interfere with the melody of life for you, remember to become still and listen.

Silence is a source of great Strength.   Unknown

First comes thought; then organization of that thought, into ideas and plans; then transformation of those plans into reality. The beginning, as you will observe, is in your imagination.   Napoleon Hill

Think Not

For I know the plans I have for you, declares the Lord, plans to prosper you, and not hurt you. Plans to give you hope and a future.
Jeremiah 29: 11

Think not, that I don't hear your prayers. I shall always!

Think not, that I don't hear your praises that glorify Me. I do hear you!

Think not, that I don't feel and know your love for Me. We are one at this time of communion!

Think not, that I have forgotten your hope for peace. Divine Love never forgets!

Think not, that I will not answer your prayers, I shall!

Think not, that I do not know of your hope and faith in me. I do!

Think not, that I never hear your concern for wholeness and wellness for you and the world. I have!

Think not, that I want anything less for you than to prosper. I have created good and abundance, for you and all. There will be no limit to the possibilities for you to progress. My good is eternal and unlimited!

I know, because it has always been in my plans. It shall happen and is happening, I am in control of it.   I AM! I AM!

Finally Brethren, whatsoever things are true, whatsoever things are honest. Whatsoever, things are just, whatsoever things are pure. Whatsoever things are lovely, whatsoever things are of good report; for if there is any virtue, and if there is any praise, **Think** *on these things.*   Philippians 4: 7–9

All major religious traditions carry basically the same message that is love, compassion and forgiveness the important thing is they should be part of our daily lives.   Dalai Lama

Peace demands the most heroic labor and the most difficult sacrifice. It demands greater heroism than war. It demands greater fidelity to the truth and a much more perfect purity of conscience. Thomas Merton

To enjoy good health to bring true happiness to one's family, to bring peace to all, one must first discipline and control one's own mind. If a man can control his mind he can find the way to Enlightenment, and all wisdom and virtue will naturally come to him.   Buddha

A true friend is someone who thinks that you are a good egg even though he knows that you are slightly cracked.   Bernard Meltzer

As you simplify your life, the laws of the universe will be simple, solitude won't be solitude, poverty will not be poverty, nor weakness be weakness.   Henry David Thoreau

The Forgiveness Factor

"I think the first step is to understand that forgiveness does not exonerate the perpetrator." Forgiveness liberates the victim. It's a gift you give yourself." Bishop T.D. Jakes

Forgiveness was one of the greatest lessons that the Master Teacher, Jesus, taught. Events take place in our lives that wound the soul. The cause of the wound can be in many forms. The wound does not have to be a blast from a weapon, spear or an arrow in the back. However, the results are the same. Hurt! It causes emotional stress, sorrow, and mistrust.

There is something so damaging about the inability to forgive, no matter the intent or cause. So, why is there such a resistance to forgive? The hurt from the perpetrator is so strong that sometimes forgiveness is difficult. Even more difficult, is to forget the event. The memory is so seared in the mind that the desire is to suppress it rather than face it. This suppression then begins the imprisonment and turmoil within the soul. There are not many who want to return to the company of the one who causes this pang within. The Master Teacher knew how the inability to let go would be, and how devastated the peace of mind and well-being on the one injured. He knew also, this one act is so important as to the joy of receiving the abundant blessings the Creator is always so willing to give us, because the unwillingness causes gridlock. The path to receiving is so congested that only the courage to move toward the freedom of forgiveness will disintegrate the sting. How is it done? The Apostle, Peter asked Jesus, "How often should one forgive those who sinned against him?" Peter said as well, "I forgive up to seven times!" Many will say, "There won't be another time, not by this same person, not to me!" "I don't let it happen to me but once!" However, when the courage rises from within us and we do move forward to release ourselves from this imprisonment, we have nothing to cause us to believe this will repeat itself. Especially from the same person! Jesus continues with His lesson to Peter, "I do not say to you seven times, but up to seventy times seven." Matthew 18: 21 – 22. Who would allow anyone cause to insult, harm, hurt, malign or disgrace them this many times? That number totals to the amount of: five hundred and forty-nine times! Who would allow oneself to repeat the experience the trauma of any situation, physically or emotionally this many times? It sounded strange to Peter and it sounds strange to us today. When we are the one desiring to be exonerated, asking once is difficult. Yet, there is no forgiveness for us when we cannot forgive others. The Master Teacher knew how obstructive the unwillingness to forgive is to our receiving the precious blessings the Father has and is so willing to give us. No matter how unsound the idea is thinking about forgiving 549 times for any offense, it is worth it to have peace of mind and the ability to move on with life. It has been said that, "It is easier to forgive a friend than to forgive oneself." It is difficult also to forget the offense. There are feelings of shame felt, and the lack of understanding why you let yourself do something so foolish. Many times others have forgiven you and forgotten, however, it is you that cannot let go. It is time that you forgive yourself as well, and move on. In the words of a great poet said it with powerful wisdom the seriousness of forgiveness; "You can't forgive without loving and I don't mean sentimentally. I don't mean mush! I mean having enough courage to stand up and say, "I forgive, I'm finished with it!" Dr. Maya Angelou. Love yourself, forgive yourself! Love others and forgive them! Don't forget to forget! If someone does not want to forgive you, love them anyway. Feel the freedom of forgiveness, and unlock the cell door that has enclosed and made you a prisoner of guilt. Use the Forgiveness Factor; it is the formula for unfailing forgiveness. Five hundred and forty-nine times (549), if necessary. Take the flight of freedom and love yourself again!

The first to Apologize is the Bravest, The first to Forgive is the Strongest, And the first to Forget is the Happiest. Author Unknown

My trust in God flows out of the experience of his loving me, day in and day out, whether the day is stormy or fair, whether I'm sick or in good health, whether I'm in a state of grace or disgrace. He comes to me where I live and loves me as I am.   Brennan Manning

Peace demands the most heroic labor and the most difficult sacrifice. It demands greater heroism than war. It demands greater fidelity to the truth and a much more perfect purity of conscience. Thomas Merton

As you simplify your life, the laws of the universe will be simple, solitude won't be solitude, poverty will not be poverty, nor weakness be weakness.   Henry David Thoreau

Happiness, true happiness, is an inner quality. It is a state of mind. If your mind is at peace, you are happy. If your mind is at peace, but you have nothing else, you can be happy. If you have everything the world can give, pleasure, possessions, power, but lack peace of mind, you can never be happy. Dada Vaswani

Every man builds his world in his own image. He has the power to choose, but no power to escape the necessity of choice.   Ayn Rand

It is hard to believe you going anywhere when you are standing still for days.   May Rose Thompson

Life: Simple or Complex?

"Life is really simple, but we insist on making it complicated." Confucius

Living a life worth living is what most people want and desire to do. How to do what is necessary to achieve it is the question. Divine Wisdom leads us to what is best to attain the maximum level of life. This Wisdom gives the desire with an idea, and a strong motivation to step forward in faith. Accepting and believing in this blessed idea with faith, starts the orderly process forward. Many things may be needed to carry out this idea. However, with the willingness to be patient and steadfast it can be done. Taking the steps in order and harmony is necessary. To some it is complicated. They get in a hurry to succeed. Why wait? Waiting is part of the willingness to allow the perfect results to have the life expected. There is a binding substance that will keep the effort together, and that is Love. Loving the idea creates all the necessity to perfect it.

In this orderly process the Creative Law of Manifestation is then demonstrated. This process works, and does not choose certain souls to enjoy a great life, it works for anyone. This is the Truth! "Truth is ever to be found in the simplicity, and not in the multiplicity and confusion of things." Isaac Newton. Life can be good, better or best, if you don't make it complicated. No good thing shall be omitted. God's pleasure is for all of us to have a good and great life. Yes! Even You! "Out of clutter, find simplicity. From discord, find harmony. In the middle of difficulty lies your opportunity. I am not a genius, I am curious. I ask many questions. And when the answers are simple. God is speaking." Albert Einstein

Live a life worth living! Love life and those in it! You deserve it! Keep it simple! There is no need to rush! To have great life is not complicated.

The adventure of life is to learn. The purpose of life is to grow. The nature of life is to changeThe challenge of life is to discover. The essence of life is to care. The opportunity of life is to serve The secret of life is to dare. The spice of life to befriend. The beauty of life is to give. Prince…the performer, composer and Instrumentalist

To live happily is a power of the soul.   Marcus Aurelius

"Peace is a gift from the Divine and I acknowledge it as such. Always begin and end your day in a peaceful state of mind through speaking and listening to God. Listening is the most important part of the process."   Wanda C. Owens

There are far too many of who place far too much stock in being alive and too little in living.   Unknown

Where I am

Where I am there is calm.
Where I am there is peace.
Where I am there is Light.
Where I am there is Love.
Where I am there is I Am
Where I am is within
And
God Is
"And lo, I Am with you always, even unto the end of the world."
Matt. 28: 20. Amen

You can try to change it, Deny it and lie about it, but in the end the Truth is still the Truth. Author Unknown

About The Author: The Reverend Dr. May Rose Thompson began her New Thought studies in 1972. Desiring to understand how to apply the studies to my life, I took more and more classes. Hearing about the 1972 May Time Retreat held at the Unity Village in Lee's Summit, Mo. She attended and it changed her life forever. In 1987, May started taking classes in Cleveland, Ohio, given by the, Universal Foundation for Better Living, Inc. founder, the Rev. Dr. Johnnie M. Colemon, Chicago, Ill. She received her teacher's license in 1992 from the, Johnnie Colemon Institute, the teaching arm of the UFBL. In 1995, she was ordained, and installed as the minister of the Living Truth Center in East Cleveland, Oh. She served on the board of UFBL for several years. Rev. May currently teaches as an associate minister at Unity Village Chapel, in Unity Village, MO. and supports the Prayer ministry there, as well as her own Alternative, ministry. Married to Ford Thompson for forty years, she has one daughter, Edwina, one, son Darrell, (deceased), and stepson, Ford Jr.

Fear not, little flock; for it is your Father's good pleasure to give you the kingdom.   Luke 12:32

God is a Spirit: and they that worship him must worship Him in Spirit and in Truth, John 4: 24. Truth: The Absolute; that which accords with God as divine principle; and ever will be; that which eternally is. Charles Fillmore...The Revealing Word

About the Author

I live in Independence, Mo. I have lived here for 15 years as of August 06. Relocating here after retiring as the Senior minister in East Cleveland Oh. for six years. I was commissioned to Interim minister by the Universal Foundation for Better Living, Inc. founder and president, Rev. Dr. Johnnie Colemon, and Ordained 1995. Served on the UFBL board for several years.

I started attending and taking lessons on Practical Christianity at Unity Centers in Cleveland, Oh. and Unity Village, Lees Summit Mo., teaching at several Unity Centers in Mo.

I have used the principles taught in these lessons since 1972. These principles changed my life.

I is my pleasure to pen as the Holy Spirit moved me that these Truth Principles do work.

Printed in the United States
By Bookmasters